My Mother's Last Field Trip:

My Encounters with God

DeJané Hill

Publisher's Note:

Spirit Led Publishing and Printing Group
Atlanta, Georgia

ISBN 978-1-7329054-7-4

9 781732 905474   51500

Cover design & Internal formatting:
Hemant Lal (AaronProductionsIndia.com)

Table of Contents

DeJane' Hill
Entrepreneur I Business Consultant I Life Coach
A Remarkable Journey of Professional Growth
Career Milestones
Visionary Entrepreneur
A Clear Vision and Sense of Purpose

Why you should read this book

By anyone's standards, I had a rough life growing up. Drugs, abusive relationships, and traumas that still bring me to tears.

But this book is not about me. I am writing this book to talk about faith and to talk about miracles. Maybe, through faith, this book will inspire you so that you too may have miracles in your life.

The book is a true story about two co-dependents: My mother and myself. How we found each other, lost each other, and found each other again in our emotional journeys together.

Fasten your seat belts.

Foreword

I have learned firsthand that the mind of a child can be a powerful thing. Little did I know that my three-year-old niece who I painfully, abet temporarily, took from my baby sister, was already beyond her years. I made this decision because I learned of the dangerous situation DeJane' was living in. A beautiful young child living with a mother who had become a slave to her drug use. So, I made the deal that I would take DeJane' for a year. But because I knew she loved her child, I told her I would give her a year to become drug-free, and then she could have her back. So DeJane' came to live with me, my husband, and our one-year-old son. DeJane' settled in quite nicely with us and we became a family. She was shy and quiet at first, but then happy and content. Then after about a year in which I believed my sister dropped the hardcore drug addiction, we returned DeJane' to her mother. However, as with some addictions, my sisters returned. After a period, my sister's addiction worsened to the point she almost lost her life to a self-inflicted drug overdose. She stated, "I could see my heart beating out my chest, so I slumped over and waited to die." This was the breaking point. Only this time, I would be taking my request before the courts and was awarded temporary custody of DeJane' at the age of 10 for two years. Once again, she came to live with us and our two boys. We were a family again.

As before, we settled into family life and DeJane' flourished. She had two little boy cousins that she adored and loved to prank, like putting clothespins on their ears and waiting until they realized it hurt to remove them. They loved each other and still do to this day. And then once again, her mother exhibited signs of being clean, so DeJane' returned to her. I did not know then that when she went back to her mother, the drug addiction was still strong and that DeJane's journey was just beginning.

In retrospect, I realized just how confusing this all had to be for DeJane'. She did not understand why she was taken from her mother and then returned, and she certainly didn't understand why after being with a "family" that she believed loved her and she loved them. Why was she being shuffled back and forth and in her mind given away, again? This led to feelings of not be wanted by the people she loved, who were supposed to love her. I realize now that when she left us the second time as a preteen, she did not understand that I also loved my sister and felt I could not keep her child from her permanently. All DeJane' saw was that I gave all her barbie dolls and accessories away after she left and to her, that was our way of saying once again, she was unwanted. But she returned to her mother and had to grow up quickly. She had to become the caretaker, the runner, the confidant, and the blocker for her mother's addiction. She did not realize during this time that the drive she had to take care of her mother, to be successful in school, to hustle for the necessities in her life were all a prelude to her future.

As a young mother myself, I had not yet gained the wisdom that age can bring. I look back and I see the young girl who although laughed and joined in on family events, sometimes she would be so quiet and still and I would jokingly say to myself "I wonder who she's talking too." I know now that her mind was active, and she was "listening." Listening to exactly what I did not know then, but I do now.

I see that the events in DeJane's young life before her mother's final transition prepared her to not just "listen", but emboldened her to seek understanding and to take action and molded her into the woman she is today. A fiercely independent woman, a nurturer who strives to be successful and the best mother she can be. A woman who has a beautiful "faith".

I hope her story and this book inspires you to set goals and achieve them by any means necessary. Letting nothing stop you from being your true self and serving God as your soul seeks and desires.

Rosella Shepherd,
Aunt & God Mother of DeJane' Hill

Early Memories

'A child's life is like a piece of paper on which every person leaves a mark." – unknown

I was born December 1, 1985, in Jackson Mississippi to an unwed nineteen-year-old single mother. My mother moved to Vicksburg before my second birthday. Until I was five, I shuttled back and forth between my maternal grandmother, Velma Hill, and my mother, Velma Brown. Going back and forth the way I did was unsettling. I never had a sense of belonging and life never seemed "normal."

By my third birthday, I was taken from my mother and given to my aunt Rosella Shepherd for one year. She recently wrote this (from the "Foreword" chapter: *Little did I know that my three-year-old niece who I painfully, abet temporarily, took from my baby sister, was already beyond her years. I made this decision because I learned of the dangerous situation DeJane' was living in. A beautiful young child living with a mother who had become a slave to her drug use.*

Back then, my mother was married to Don Brown, her first husband, and not a genuinely nice man. They divorced when I was four and then my mother remarried Lamont Brown by the time I was five. It was a strange set of circumstances. When Lamont entered our lives, the shuttling back and forth stopped. I was disoriented, confused, and not old enough to figure out why. Being an only child, I had no sibling to chat with or compare notes. I was on my own and adrift with Lamont being my caretaker.

My Vicksburg family in those days consisted of my mother, my grandmother, my aunt, and my uncle.

Other aunts and uncles were around, but not living in Vicksburg.

My life started to change when I entered first grade. I had a teacher, friends, and a new life outside of my unsettled family life. I was an intelligent child and the teacher's pet, although having the attention that went with being the teacher's pet was "a negative." It was not cool to have the teacher's attention; you lost friends, and this affected me later in life. I was a victim of bullying, felt alone, and was ashamed of being "wise."

The element of faith was largely missing in my life. My only exposure to faith was through my grandmother; she had always stressed the importance of faith. My grandmother's words on faith were lost on me, to an extent. I could not relate her words to me or my life. That had to come later when I was more mature. I was not conscious enough to understand, so it made me want to "know more."

My Mother's Truth, My Secret

"One of the most important relationships we have is the relationship with our mothers." – *Iyanla Vanzant*

I was in the second grade. It is only now that I understand that my mother was disabled and unable to work because of prior brain surgery. I learned later that she was addicted to drugs, crack cocaine specifically. I was embarrassed about this and did not want to discuss it with anyone. Much of the time I was alone while my mother was hiding her habit from the others in my family, including my stepfather. I lived with, my aunt briefly; she was aware of the addiction problem but not of the severity. My family had no

11

presence in my mother's home life, and they were busy living their own lives, and, unfortunately, my mother's truths were being swept under the rug.

I need to make several important points here. My mother was addicted to drugs, but she was still my mother. I lacked for nothing materially; I was even spoiled. She was a "functioning mother", but, perhaps because of her addiction, she was incapable of developing an emotional and nurturing attachment to me. I know she loved me as any mother loves any child.

My relationship with my mother was strained. I felt that she loved me only because I was her child, not for who I was. I was filled with self-doubts and that, in turn, blocked "my gift" and my exposure to faith.

Lamont Brown, my stepfather, was like "a double-edged sword." He was my saving grace but also a person that enabled my mother's habit. I was happy

to have a "father figure", but he was more of a friend than a parent. His presence in my life allowed me to function better, go to school, and "not miss a beat" because he was always home. Believe it or not, I was a spoiled child in those days; he provided everything I needed and much more.

Although it shames me to admit it, even I enabled my mother from time to time. Lamont would sometimes not have enough money to feed my mother's habit, so I might give her something of mine that had value (such as jewelry) to pawn and send her on her way. She always promised to return the items to me "in time", but those promises sometimes failed. Lamont would find out about this and they would argue, so that this, my enabling, became "my little secret" with my mother.

I felt a responsibility towards my mother. I wanted her home with me. So, while I sometimes enabled her habit, I was, in many ways, her caretaker and playing her "mother" in a weird role reversal. I cooked meals and was in an adult role not of my choosing. I was "a fixer", trying to fix the world around me at that time.

As you will see later in my story, all of these experiences, coupled with my evolving faith, really strengthened my resolve and shaped me into a much better person and a proficient "life coach."

The Conflicts

"If a girl is silent or distant... she's either over thinking, tired of waiting, about to blow up, needs a hug, falling apart, crying inside, or all of the above." – unknown

The pre-teen and teenage years are difficult for anyone and they were certainly all of that for me. I harbored a great amount of anger. When I was ten, my mother sent me over to live with my aunt, Rosella Shepherd, in Texas for the second time, "so that she could become clean." She even went as far as giving custodial rights to my aunt. The becoming clean never happened. I resented my family members during "the shuffle" and felt angry and abandoned.

When I returned to my mother almost two years later, I was twelve and my mother was still in the grip of her drug habit. I had been away from my home, but for what purpose? My anger swelled up inside. I still loved my mother, but I did not like her. Not one bit. I was emotionally connected to my mother because she was my mother, otherwise, I felt a blinding hatred.

The hatred bubbled and boiled. My mother was controlling and trying to be a "now" mom. One day my mother attacked me, stated that I was being "rebellious", and started a fistfight. My mother had me arrested and handed me over to juvenile detention for two days. When this happened, all my love left me. My stepfather was calling the shots and my mother was catering to his needs while ignoring mine.

Those years (thirteen to fifteen) were extremely rocky. The only good news during this period is that my mother stopped her addiction and became clean. Maybe that had something to do with her then trying to be the perfect mother and controlling my life. Teenagers never like to be controlled. Yes, I get that. But the resentment I felt was because of both my mother's controlling nature and my tumultuous past.

In my older teen years, fifteen to seventeen, I ran away to live with two different aunts from time to time. I had been dating and, when I was seventeen, my mother (more my stepfather, drowning out my mother's voice) threw me out of the house and told me to move in with my boyfriend while I was still in high school Remember my saying that my stepfather was "a double-edged sword?" Well, I got one blade of his sword and was shipped out

Then, making a bad thing worse a few months after moving in, our home was burglarized, and my boyfriend shot and killed our neighbor. Not wanting to be associated in any way with the incident of the neighbor and for my safety, my mother suggested I leave the boyfriend's apartment and move in with my biological father in Phoenix Arizona. I had to leave during the last semester of my senior year in high school. I had to balance the fear of not graduating with my being scared for my life.

That did not last long. I learned that my father was "a crack head" also. He up and left just one day after I arrived!

What was I to do now? I had known all my life that I had a half-brother "Juicy", living in Phoenix. I temporarily moved in with my brother's child's mother's home.

My brother discussed our father's addiction and explained to me why he, my father, had never been a part of my life – he wanted me to be out of his care and in the care of my new stepfather. From that point on, my brother became the father figure in my life although I was just eighteen and my brother twenty-one or twenty-two.

My brother was good to me but, after a month or so, I returned home and found a place of my own in Vicksburg Mississippi. I finished high school while in Vicksburg and reunited with my boyfriend for the next few years until his prison sentence began.

I dropped out of college, was disconnected from my family, and decided to leave. At nineteen I felt abandoned and alone. I had no financial support. I was into a deep clinical depression that I did not know would last for years to come. I moved to Gulfport Mississippi. I lived there until I was twenty-one and then moved back to Vicksburg. I fell in love, married Anthony Cleveland, and had my first child, Aidyn D'nae Cleveland when I was twenty-two. We moved to Texas a year later and I was finally happy; my first child gave me a sense of genuine love.

But depression worsened. I was severely depressed and hospitalized. We returned to Mississippi and we divorced a few years later when I was twenty-six. I was

19

now a single mom and very lost. I was determined not to fail my daughter as my mother had failed me.

The Curse Returns

"Death and life are in the power of the tongue."

– Proverbs 18:21

What I did not mention earlier is that my mother had a tumor on her brain since I was one year old. They operated on the brain back then and took out all but one inoperable piece. That piece remained for all these years, applying increasing pressure on the vital parts of her brain. There was always the fear, voiced by my grandmother, that the tumor might grow back, although I did not know much more about the tumor or its effects.

Twenty plus years later, on my advice, and after my mother's memory was fading, I convinced my mother to go with me to the doctor and have the tumor checked out. I had had some medical training in addition to my business training and I suspected that something was not right. Although my mother had had checkups every year, this time the tumor had indeed returned, or at least had grown and had become a more aggressive tumor the size of an adult fist, presumed to be cancerous because of its size.

I was older and wiser now. I began to reflect on what my mother's tumor had meant in all these prior years. The tumor was laying on her hypothalamic and pineal glands, so one consequence was that she could not have any other children while another consequence was that it prevented her from developing and nurturing her faith. Those factors could be attributed to her tumor, but other factors were contributing to my mother's unhappiness: She was dealing with the loss of her father since she had been thirteen. Her husband of twenty years, my atheist stepfather had been cheating on her. He was mentally abusive. They argued a great deal. I began to understand how difficult it must have been for my mother to deal with all this and try to be "the perfect mom." I understood all of this now, as an adult. This revelation came about because of my spiritual development and my relationship with God.

My stepfather was nonchalant about all of this. This saddened me because my mother had always been there for him during his illnesses, self-inflicted by his severe alcoholism. They had life insurance, he would get some money, so what was the problem? The doctors so far had advised that the tumor was inoperable, she would lose her motor functions and die. She would lose her mind and might even forget me.

We got an appointment for a second opinion with a different doctor. This doctor stated that it was a miracle for my mother to have the tumor in her brain for the past twenty-five years. He was amazed that she lived and functioned well until now. His diagnosis: "She is fearful but brave."

I asked one hundred questions. Only God knew what would happen next. "In God we trust", but would that trust end in my mother's death? My mother's only question was "Will I die?"

With a glimmer of hope in my heart, I started the role reversal that was necessary for my mother. I would become the mother, the caretaker, and my newly acquired faith would get both of us through this. I had a good job and I was about to be transferred to a new position in Texas, but I felt that my calling was staying with my mother and made that difficult (but prayerful) choice.

Shortly after my mother was diagnosed with an aggressive tumor, my best friend, Tatiana Hunt was diagnosed with stage four aggressive cervical cancer. Like my mother, Tatiana was fearful but brave.

I had never experienced anyone with cancer before, but now my two closest relationships, my mother and my best friend, were being ravaged. I asked God, "Who are you going to take first?" and "How can I be there for both?" I was putting on my armor for war.

God gave me strength. I tried being as positive as I could. Seeing Tatiana suffer may have saved my life – I became, more aware of my health and became far more health-conscious. Tatiana passed away peacefully, the way that she wanted - my first experience with the death of someone close. Tatiana still visits me in my dreams to this day. I feel her energy daily. (She is the angel who watches over me.)

Tatiana inspired me. I watched her mend relationships and I wanted to do the same, especially

with my mother. Tatiana always quoted "What God
has for me is for me!"

My Encounter with the Voice of God

"For we walk by faith, not by sight…"

− 2 Corinthians 5:7

Not everyone converses with God the same way. In my time of need, God whispered to me in a gentle (but sharp) voice. The voice I heard was a source of revelations and had a clarity of focus.

I asked God who would die first, my best friend, or my mother. I was in a rocky relationship, recently divorced, and wanting to move out of town. So many things were going on. I just wanted to escape. I was confused, depressed, and conflicted. I strongly needed God's guidance.

My best friend passed, and I missed her terribly. Should I move? Should I care for my mother 24/7 or should I leave her with my stepfather? It was at this time that God started speaking with me. My daughter was young and did not understand why I was an emotional wreck. I went into a quiet corner while my daughter was napping and began to cry. Suddenly, I heard Tatiana's voice. She said, "Dookie, I'm okay." She said it twice.

I knew that it was Tatiana speaking as "Dookie" was her private expression for me. I also knew that she had landed safely in heaven. I was not close to God before my hearing Tatiana's voice, but hearing her voice made me realize that God WAS there for me and we needed to talk. And all of that told me that I needed to unselfishly focus on my mother.

I was visiting my mother in her home as best as I could, given my work schedule. But my mother was getting weaker; she was not able to stand or walk very well. She sometimes lay in a pool of urine. My mother was not properly cared for by my stepfather. I felt he was the enemy who delightfully enjoyed seeing my mother's health decline.

I went to see my mother to pick her up for Thanksgiving dinner and when I arrived, she did not answer the door but answered the phone. She told me that she could not move. I panicked, telling my mother that I was going home for a spare key, three minutes up the road. I prayed and asked God to please get her to the door; I would do the rest. God said, "Go back now." When I returned, my mother staggered to the door.

I brought my mother into my home and decided to ramp up my role as a caretaker. It was not working with my stepfather! Anger swelled up in my and I had a vision of killing my stepfather. I was in the bathtub and crying. God recognized that I was in my weakest moment. He whispered to me: **"When you are at your weakest, I am at my strongest."**

Later, as I watched my mother sitting on her couch, God said to call her name (There was no response). He said to dial her phone number. My mother never noticed her phone ringing. He said to walk around her, but she never focused on me.

The journey deepened. I was pregnant with my second child and ending a toxic relationship when I next heard the voice of God. At this time, my mother was unable to walk, talk, or feed herself. My mother's home care from that time included hospital equipment, home therapy, intimate hygiene care, and other costs.

All of this showed me the extent to which my mother's life was at home and how she was fast declining.

God spoke in a gentle, soothing but sharp voice: **"I prepared you for this!"** He had my full attention!

The Rescue

"Hope is the expectation that something outside of ourselves, something or someone external, is going to come to our rescue and we will live happily ever after."

– Dr. Robert Anthony

It was early in January of 2014. We had no general practitioner, so I was doing the best that I could without that form of guidance.

It got to the point where my mother could not talk and could not move, so I rushed her to the hospital.

My mother was severely dehydrated. Although we had been to the hospital several times before, this time was different. This was the time when an on-call surgeon read her chart, called me outside the room, and said that there was a chance (50/50) that he could remove the tumor successfully.

I started to pray in earnest. I told my mother that the doctor had said that he felt there was a "50/50 chance" by "the grace of God" that he could remove the tumor and bring my mother back to good health. We prayed for my mother's full restoration. 50-50 was much better than a death sentence, so we took him up on his offer and scheduled an operation after I asked the doctor "one hundred questions."

My mother was forty-eight as was the surgeon. The surgeon said that "At forty-eight, I could not see passing at this age. 50/50 is much better than zero."

No other surgeon wanted to take on this task, but he would. God had to be at work here. Our surgeon, Dr. Adams, was "the chosen one."

As it turned out, this surgeon had performed similar operations several times, was an expert, and had written a book about it. Luck or providence?

I told my mother that the tumor could not go where she was going (heaven); it would have to be removed and stay right here on earth. I felt that God wanted her "whole" again.

What did this miracle accomplish? We had hope. My prayers had been answered. I had a purpose in my life, helping my mother. If my mother were to leave me, I would know that I was loved as a child. I was whole. It was no longer about me; it was about her. The hate that I felt as a child washed away. I was filled with love. With my medical experience, I could speak with the doctors on her behalf with confidence

Although the situation was potentially horrible, I was filled with God's glory and I was at peace and prepared.

Our Journey as One

"If you can't fly, then run. If you can't run, then walk. If you can't walk, then crawl, but by all means, keep moving." – M. L. King Jr.

The first surgery was scheduled for January 4th but got delayed until January 17th. I never questioned the delay.

The operation was, in one sense, a complete success. Whereas before, every surgeon felt that her remaining tumor was inoperable, this doctor completely removed the tumor.

There was, however, and because of the tumor's large size, pressure on the brain, and extensive residual damage to the brain tissue. My mother was left in a "medically" vegetative state. She remained in a long-term care facility for what they called "rehab."

The doctors had given up hope; they said she was still unresponsive. Then, after a few months, I noticed that my mother was watching my daughter. I worked with her and got her to blink in response to questions and move her right arm/hand to communicate. I began to do the range of motion and other techniques to get her arms to move. Finally, she learned to communicate non-verbally with me and with others.

I used to refer to her visits to the hospital as "field trips" because I worked full-time and was a single mom. Although my mother was thirty minutes away, I would try to visit her every day, but could not be there for every routine doctor visit. Dr. Adam's nurse would call me if she felt it was important that I visit;

I also signed the necessary permission for ambulance transportation.

With that in mind, this was the start of a journey into the unknown. Would my mother ever recover? What was going to happen and when? I was now the mother in charge of my mother, again in a role reversal.

I had a myriad of personal feelings affecting me during these difficult times. I was battling my own demons with being single and pregnant with my second child. I had financial woes. I was alone, scared, but brave.

There were several more post-surgery trips to the hospital, I would work and plan to arrive before any scheduled doctor visits or surgery. My mother would be transported for her appointments by ambulance.

During these visits, my mother could hear my voice but was unable to talk. I would tell my mother where she was going and for what purpose. I would tell her that I would be waiting for her when she returned. She was going on a "field trip" and I, acting as her mother and caretaker, would be there when she came back.

The Last Field Trip, The Rite of Passage

"Your pain is a divine rite of passage through which you will be reborn as a being of strength, wisdom, and purpose." – Bryant McGill

It was April 13th, 2015, and I was at work when I received a from the emergency room. There had been an incident and my mother had been rushed there.

I called my grandmother, told her that I would get there as soon as possible, and asked her to meet me in the hospital.

My grandmother called me right back. Something was different this time. I raced thirty miles to the hospital. When I entered my mother's room, she was looking at me, her face contorted in pain. Her face said, "I told you I wanted no pain and I am hurting right now."

My mother had power of attorney and I was told just to keep her out of pain and not to administer anything. She already had had a feeding tube and a tracheostomy for fifteen months at that time.

My mother had never complained in any of the previous surgeries. The doctor said, however, that this must hurt "like hell"; it is just that she cannot speak.

The doctor further advised that my mother was on life support and had zero chance of any quality of life. I now had the painful task to summon my bravery and relay the sad news to my grandmother and the rest of the family.

I was able to have some form of communication with my mother, although it was different this time. I would talk and she would respond by blinking or by facial movements. I told my mother that she was on life support and things were very bad for her. She managed to smile, albeit contorted.

When I tried to explain further what was going on, my mother looked at me with a puzzled look, as if to say, "What do you mean?" I told her that there was good news. She would now have an opportunity to visit her grandmother and her father. My mother understood. She smiled her crooked smile when I mentioned her father. It was my mother's last field trip and my mother accepted it without hesitation.

This was my last conscious talk with my mother, and she knew it was okay to die. I told her to go to sleep that night and tell God that you are ready for Him. My mother accepted her fate.

I permitted the hospital to "pull the plug" and let her pass peacefully.

I waited by her bedside with other family members. I was excited because I wanted to be there to hear her last words, to "speak" to me. I knew that she would speak to me; I knew from my prayers.

After about an hour. My mother would talk a long breath and let it out. Take another long breath and let it out, muttering what sounded like "uh uh", speaking in vibrations. My mother then began to snore and slept eleven more days! During the early morning of her transition, after my normal prayer, I recall saying: "Mom, I can stay with you until tomorrow." My Aunt Rose was in town and with my children. I was finally able to stay overnight.

I fell asleep and was later awakened by a nurse who said that my mother had stopped breathing. My thoughts then were simple, "Thank God, she suffers no more." I know now that my mother did not want me to experience waking up and finding her not breathing. She was a "private person" and wanted to transition "solo."

Mom died on April 30th, 2015.

The eleven days were a blessing. I had the time to prepare her funeral and, more importantly, prepare myself mentally. Everything ran smoothly, the funeral and all the arrangements. The number eleven is also significant in that it took me eleven days to write this book.

Now, five years later, I am a different woman. I have transformed myself, with God's help, into a thoughtful, giving person. I can help others and do so professionally as a "life coach." My mother's last field trip and the last five years have been my rite of passage into the person I am today.

The Prayer that Changed my Life

"Faith does not make things easy; it makes them possible." – Luke 1:37

After my mother's passing, I had many questions that needed to be answered. No longer a caretaker/ mother surrogate, what is my next mission. More importantly, did my mother reach heaven?

One night I put my petitions out there before God and my answer came back in a dream. I saw my mother's smiling face in the clouds, and I knew that she was safe and sound in her new home and thankful, with big cheeks, red lipstick, and fierce eyebrows. I was comforted. I was at peace. I had no regrets and was able to move forward.

Later that year, I prayed and asked God "for something to do." I had started my first business: event planning ("Posh Events by DeJane'"). "Posh Events" was a business created for me by God. I was shocked at my success because I had never known anyone who started their own business. I felt free to express and create. I had a beginning sense of what I wanted to become. This was the "something to do" that God had given me. I was able to mold all my skill sets into a successful business.

I enjoyed this work, but I wanted to do something for others, leveraging all my recent experiences

I let my prayers guide me when I listened to God's voice (not always). I knew that God was guiding me but, in the beginning, I was unable to understand His "end game." I made many contacts, learned a great deal, and was, in my view, being prepared for something greater and more meaningful.

In 2016, I moved to Atlanta Georgia with my two children. I did not want to return to "what I was." Rather, I just wanted God's continued guidance. I was busy planting my seeds to see how they might grow.

The Enlightenment

"For I know the plans I have for you, plans to prosper you and not harm you, plans to give you hope and a future." – *Jeremiah 29:11*

The question still lingered: "What do I want to do with my life?" I had moved to Georgia to renew myself and find direction. What should I be doing? Should I be seeking my life partner? What did I want and what did God want for me? I struggled. Some of my demons were trying to push me in directions away from God's will. My journey needed to be with God, not my own, and not one misdirected by my demons.

Then, at thirty-three, I looked back on my life and saw how the pieces fell together. I was in a prayer relationship with God, feeling His hand in my career transitions and I had started my mission of turning people's pain into passions. It was like me seeing a beautiful patchwork quilt, woven by God, come together. The quilt, my life, was in plain view in front of me. I could purge myself of my doubts and insecurities. My next mission had started.

Jesus did amazing things in his life before he died at age thirty-three. I was thirty-three, as was Jesus, and it was time to fulfill MY mission with Jesus as my big brother.

My early negative memories faded, along with my false belief systems. I no longer need therapy. I loved and was loved by others. I had broken away from family curses. I now had a purpose, revealed by my past experiences. I was on my next journey as a "master healer."

My future mattered. Lives mattered. I mattered.

Gratitude

- To My Mother, Madame Renee, I dedicate my entire life to you. You're the reason I'm such a brave woman; I'm grateful you gave me you all and even what you couldn't – God had your back. I remember you telling me I couldn't save the world – I replied, I'll die trying – now that's starting not to seem so far out fetched with the strength you instilled within me. Our time together was far from perfect, but you trained me to love – so I'll honor you by "loving others as I want to be loved." We both know personally from our journey as one that – love conquers everything. I thank God daily for allowing me to enter this world through such a brave woman's womb in which he provided you. Hope I'm making you proud, Rest in Royalty Momz!

- Tatiana! My best sister gal friend ever – your vibrant energy still radiates in my life daily – you make sure of that through various channels. When they saw friends to the end – your picture is there. From secrets, laughs, fears, and more...you remained a true friend until we departed. We shared a special connection while you were in here and still to this day in spirit – you still provide your "two cents" when I truly need it - you're my angel and I honor you!

- My Why's – Aidyn and Ashton, affectionately known as King to his loved ones – he is named after my mother's father. You both are the same and different in many ways, but one thing is consistent, you both are the reasons I strive to be the best I can be for you. I pray for you both to keep God first and allow Him in your lives to carry you into all things impossible. I love you both more than life itself and I'm grateful to be able to watch you grow into loving, respectable God-fearing adults.

- My Greatest Love Ever – is you, Mr. Johnny Brantley – the love we share is one of a kind and can never be replaced. You've pushed me into new levels of this thing called "womanhood" and I've personally learned more about myself through our relationship than anything else. For that I'm forever grateful to you – I've also very proud of the growth you've shown through our years together. Thank you for being authentic with me and when things I said "didn't make any sense to you" – thanks for still supporting and encouraging me. Life surely isn't perfect, but making lemonade with our beautiful lemons is our "picture-perfect" ending. I love you; it's only up from here – I'm honored to be a partner with you in this thing called life.

- Aaron "Juicy" Wilson – what do I say – my first love, my support, my inner twin, my solider, and ammunition in any war - I want to thank you for always having my back! And for telling me the raw truth as the big brother should always do. Thank you for not only being the best big brother but for stepping in and being my father as well. I recall you buying me shoes when I was in elementary and you had to only been in high school at the time because our "donor" failed, as usual, another holiday as usual. God placed us together for a reason – ying and yang twins! A force to reckon with and an unbreakable bond – I'm proud of you – you're what we didn't have – A GREAT FATHER! I love you with every breath in me!

- To my grandmother, Velma Hill, Aunts, and the rest of my family – I want to thank you for supporting me and loving me through everything life has thrown our way. Thanks for listening to me for hours share my visions, dreams, and aspirations since a young child. Grandmother, I truly thank you for teaching me about faith and instilling in me a spirit of God at an early age. I love you all!

- My Circle of Sisters – what would I do without each of every one of you! You ladies mean so much to me; being an only kid in the home growing up – I've always wanted sisters! God filled me with more than enough sisters to share and experience this life with; Sharron we entered the wombs together and I'm very grateful for our bond over the years. Nadia – thanks for never missing a beat! Turkessa – always love from the beginning to the end! Stephanie and Naeasea – best big sisters ever

– thank you for always "telling me right!" Kanika, "we started from the bottom, now we here – love you, hun!" Tori, Meka, Toya, Shantel – BFFs 4Life! Keniysha – girl, your heaven sent! I love you all; mentioned and not.

- The Bro-Hood – Walter and Maurice! I love you guys dearly! Every girl needs a right and a left-hand man – and I got just that! I meet you both when I was 12 years old, and you both instantly became my big brothers. I've adored you both since then and even more now – seeing you grow into men and fathers; it's been an honor. Thanks for believing in me, supporting me, and being the "men", I needed during difficult times in my life.

- To my mentor, business coach, and friend - Dr. Velma Trayham – I am truly am grateful for you and how God has allowed you to help shift things around in my life. I never knew the value a mentor would provide until I was introduced to you – and immediately I begin to pray about the reason God had brought to us together. He truly blessed me when he sat us at the same table – he promised "your gift will make room for you," Proverbs 18:16 – thank you for believing in my vision and pushing me into my greatness - my sister in Soul – I love you! The MMA Family – I love you and grateful for each one of you – you ladies inspire me!

To all my supporters along my journey, my teachers who taught me many lessons, and spiritual advisors who showed me the greater than is within me - I want to say thank you and I love you all! You are forever in my heart and spirit. Forever grateful for all your support.

"There are only two ways to live your life –
One is as though nothing is a miracle,
And the other is as though everything is a miracle."
~ Albert Einstein

Biography

DeJane' Hill

Entrepreneur | Business Consultant | Life Coach

DeJane' Hill is an enthusiastic and infectious entrepreneur, business consultant, and life coach. She is currently the founder and CEO of Posh Events, an innovative event-planning, and specialty services company based in Atlanta, Georgia.

Started in 2015, Posh Events has helped numerous clients across Atlanta with wildly imaginative event design and planning concepts. Hill and her team have worked with distinguished clients to plan weddings, corporate events, and parties. Over the past five years, her business has expanded into numerous markets.

"Change your thinking process, and you change the process of your life"
– DeJane' Hill -

A Remarkable Journey of Professional Growth

Hill has been a catalyst for growth, change, and corporate success for top organizations that range from international manufacturing & supply companies and non-profit agencies to healthcare providers. Her management and leadership skills have carried her across the spectrum of enterprise-level corporate environments over the past 20 years.

DeJane' Hill's coaching initiative, One Life, One Creation, has empowered hundreds of women, as they discover their true potential and establish their life goals. She has guided numerous women who are on the path to healing and self-discovery. Her efforts have created opportunities and clear benchmarks for others to follow in their lives and careers.

Career Milestones

DeJane' Hill earned her business degree from American Intercontinental University. Other notable credentials include:
- Successful implementation and restructuring of internal processes for enterprise-level organizations
- Fundraising strategy development and execution that has generated over $500K monthly in donations.
- Certified Transformational Life Coach, helping women achieve their personal and professional goals

Visionary Entrepreneur

Each moment throughout DeJane' career prepared her for the launch of Posh Events, a comprehensive event planning company that serves clients in Atlanta, Ga and throughout the U.S. Posh Events provides a wide range of customized services such as event planning, decor, vendor sourcing, catering, rentals, layout & design, and full event execution.

DeJane' Hill and her team have a collaborative spirit, working closely with the client through each stage of the event planning process. Her meticulous attention to detail, impeccable work ethic, and ability to identify and recruit talented individuals are what have fueled the success of Posh Events.

A Clear Vision and Sense of Purpose

DeJane' Hill understands the importance of self-improvement and helping others become the best version of themselves. She is guided by a core principle: love others as you want to be loved. She also knows what it takes to fight for what is important. Her goal is to empower those around her and embrace positive vibrant energy that nurtures her life, her brand, and her companies.

ISBN 978-1-7329054-7-4

51500

Lightning Source UK Ltd.
Milton Keynes UK
UKHW020637170720
366698UK00015B/1731